Low-Carb Essentials Cookbook

Low-Carb Recipes You'll Love to Cook

Jamie S. Garner

Table Of Contents

Jill Boelsma's Scottish Eggs

This is a decarbed version of what is actually a classic recipe. Our tester, Ray,

called this "fabulous!" and when asked ifhe'd make it again, answered with a

hearty "Oh, yeah! "

4 hard-boiled eggs

1 pound (455 g) Jimmy Dean or other bulk breakfast sausage

Spicy pork rinds, crushed

Preheat oven to 350°F (180°C).

Peel your hard-boiled eggs.

Divide the sausage into 4 equal portions and flatten each into a thin patty

between your palms. Encase each hard-boiled egg in sausage by slowly wrapping

a patty around it; then roll in pork rind crumbs. Place on a cookie sheet you've

sprayed with nonstick cooking spray, and bake for 20 to 25 minutes.

Yield: 4 servings

Each with: 577 calories; 52 g fat; 23 g protein; 2 g carbohydrate;

0 g dietary fiber; 2 g usable carbs.

Jody's Breakfast Wrap

Our tester, Julie, now calls this recipe "a low-carb staple."

1 or 2 strips bacon

1-2 eggs

1 low-carb tortilla

2-3 tablespoons (20-30 g) shredded cheese-cheddar or Monterey Jack

are good

First, you need to deal with the bacon and the scrambled eggs. I'd microwave the bacon-lay it on a microwave bacon rack or in a glass pie plate, and nuke it on high (a minute per slice is about right in my microwave, but microwaves vary).

Keep an eye on it the first couple of times, and you'll get the timing down. Drain your bacon on a paper towel while you scramble the eggs.

You can scramble your egg or eggs plain or add a splash of cream if you like. Just beat 'em up in a bowl. Spray a medium skillet with nonstick cooking spray, and add a little butter if you want to. Heat over medium-high flame, pour in the eggs, and scramble till set.

Lay your low-carb tortilla on a microwaveable plate. Sprinkle the cheese on it, and microwave on high for 10 to 20 seconds-you just want to melt the cheese. Add the scrambled egg and bacon, roll it up, and enjoy!

Tester's note: Julie says the eggs and bacon can even be made ahead and put into a plastic snap-top container, and then used for a couple of days in a row for a fast and easy breakfast on the go. Just nuke the bacon and egg separately (it needs more nuke time than the tortilla), nuke the tortilla with the cheese, com bine, and go. Breakfast made in less than a minute, and totally portable for the

commute to work!

Yield: 1 serving

Made with 2 eggs and 3 tablespoons (30 g) of cheese, this has: 254 calories;

17 g fat; 20 g protein; 12 g carbohydrate; 8 g dietary fiber; 4 g usable carbs.

Sharon Walsh's Mushroom-Spinach Egg-Muffin Thing or Something Like That

That's the name my husband gave this recipe, and I liked it so much, I kept it!

Whatever you call it, it's a great breakfast or supper!

4 eggs and '/2 cup (120 ml) egg whites or 6 eggs

'/2 10-ounce (280 g) package frozen chopped spinach, thawed

and well drained

'/2 cup (50 g) finely chopped fresh mushrooms

'/2 cup (60 g) shredded cheddar

'/2 cup (60 g) shredded mozzarella

'/2 cup (115 g) ricotla cheese

1 tablespoon (10 g) minced onion

1 tablespoon (5 g) Mrs. Dash (or other seasoning mix)

1 tablespoon (10 g) chopped garlic

1 teaspoon salt or Vege-Sal

'/4 teaspoon pepper

Preheat your oven to 350°F (180°C). Spray a 12-cup muffin tin with nonstick

cooking spray.

Whisk up your eggs in a mixing bowl. Add the vegetables, cheeses, and season   ings, and mix thoroughly. Spoon into the prepared muffin cups and bake for 20

to 25 minutes or until brown, puffy, and set.

Note: Sharon says these can be made ahead and reheated in your microwave for

a quick breakfast or lunch. She likes turkey bacon on the side!

Yield: 4 servings, 3 muffins each.

Each serving has: 269 calories; 19 g fat; 20 g protein; 5 g carbohydrate;

1 g dietary fiber, 4 g usable carbs.

Swiss Puff

This is a great comfort-food-type supper.

4 eggs

3/4 teaspoon salt or Vege-Sal

'/2 teaspoon pepper

1 tablespoon (15 g) butter

1 batch Ultimate Fauxtatoes (page 136)

2 cups (240 g) shredded Swiss cheese

4 scallions, sliced, including the crisp part of the green shoot

2 tablespoons (10 g) chopped parsley

4 drops hot sauce

Separate your eggs. (Since whites with even a tiny speck of yolk in them will stubbornly refuse to whip up, do yourself a favor and separate each egg into a small cup or bowl.) Dump the yolks into the Fauxtatoes and beat them in; add the salt, pepper, and butter. Dump your (presumably yolkless) egg whites into a deep mixing bowl and set aside.

Stir the shredded Swiss cheese into the Fauxtatoes, then stir in the scallions, parsley, and hot sauce.

Now, using an electric mixer, beat the whites until they stand in soft peaks. Fold gently into the Fauxtatoes. Spoon the whole thing into a 6-cup (1.4 L) casserole you've sprayed with nonstick cooking spray. Bake for 40 to 45 minutes at 375 °F (190°C).

Yield: 4 to 5 servings

Assuming 4 servings, each will have: 422 calories; 25 g fat; 32 g protein; 18 g carbohydrate; 8 g dietary fiber; 10 g usable carbs.

Jill Taylor's Chili Relleno Casserole

Love Mexican food? I do! Here's a great Mexican-style casserole. Since traditional Chilies Rellenos is delicious but labor-intensive, this is a really great alternative.

2-3 roasted green chilies

'/2 pound (225 g) sharp cheddar, finely shredded

8 ounces (225 g) salsa

'/2 pound (225 g) Monterey Jack, finely shredded

5 eggs

1 cup (240 ml) whipping cream

Preheat oven to 350°F (180°C).

Chop your green chilies and spread half of them in the bottom of a 9" x 13" (22.5 x 32.5 cm) casserole dish you've sprayed with nonstick cooking spray.

Spread the cheddar evenly over the chilies, then pour the salsa over the top.

Add the Monterey Jack, then top with the remaining green chilies.

In a mixing bowl, beat the eggs and cream until combined and pour over the

chilies and cheese. Bake at 350°F (180°C) for approximately 1 hour or until set.

Serve with green salad as a light lunch or as a side with your favorite entree.

Jill's note: "Do not use a dish that is smaller but deeper. The result is better

when the casserole rises to about 2" (5 cm) in height."

Yield: 10 servings

Each will have: 301 calories; 25 g fat (75.6% calories from fat); 15 g protein;

4 g carbohydrate; trace dietary fiber; 4 g usable carbs.

Zucchini Bread

Many low carbers tell me they miss having "a little

something" with a cup of

coffee or tea for breakfast, and express a profound

weariness with eggs. Here's

something for you! This Zucchini Bread is moist,

sweet, cinnamon-y, and deli   cious-not to mention

being low carb and having as much protein per slice

as a

couple of eggs!

'/2 cup (120 ml) canola oil

'/4 cup (85 g) sugar-free imitation honey

2 eggs

'/3 cup (80 g) plain yogurt

1 cup (125 g) pumpkin seed meal (see page 24)

1 cup (125 g) vanilla whey protein powder

1 V2 teaspoons baking soda

'/2 teaspoon salt

1 teaspoon cinnamon

'/3 cup (18 g) Splenda granular

1 cup (125 g) chopped walnuts

1 V2 cups (180 g) shredded zucchini (about one 6"
[15 cm] zucchini)

Preheat the oven to 350°F (180 0

().

In a good-sized mixing bowl, combine the oil,
imitation honey, eggs, and yogurt.

Whisk these together. Now, in a second bowl,
measure the dry ingredients: the

ground pumpkin seeds, vanilla whey protein powder,
baking soda, salt, cinnamon,

and Splenda. Stir them together, making sure any
little lumps of baking soda get

broken up. Now whisk the dry ingredients into the
wet ingredients. Stir just until

everything is well combined; no need for prolonged
beating. Finally, stir in the

walnuts and the shredded zucchini, mixing well.

Pour into a loaf pan you've sprayed well with
nonstick cooking spray-my loaf pan

is large, 5" x 9" (13 x 22.5 cm). Bake for about 50 minutes, or until a toothpick

inserted into the center comes out clean. Turn out onto a wire rack for cooling.

Yield: About 16 slices

Each with: 194 calories; 14 g fat, 14 g protein; 5 g carbohydrate; 2 g dietary

fiber-for a usable carb count of just 3 g a slice. (arb count does not include

polyols in the sugar-free imitation honey.

Cranberry Nut Muffins

I tried Cranberry Nut Bread, and it was a failure-all the cranberries rose, so the

top of the bread was soggy. But muffins worked out fine!

1/2 cup (60 g) pecans

1/2 cup (50 g) cranberries

3/4 cup plus 2 tablespoons (110 g) almond meal

3/4 cup (90 g) vanilla whey protein powder

2 tablespoons (30 g) gluten

2 tablespoons (30 g) polyol

1/4 cup (6 g) Splenda

2 V2 teaspoons baking powder

2 eggs

3/4 cup (180 ml) carb Countdown Dairy Beverage

3 tablespoons (45 g) butter, melted

1/4 teaspoon orange extract

Preheat your oven to 400°F (200°C). Spray a 12-cup muffin tin with nonstick cooking spray, or line it with paper muffin cups if you prefer.

Chop your pecans, then your cranberries-I do them by pulsing the S-blade of

my food processor, and if you do them in this order, you won 't have pecans stick   ing to the moisture left behind by the cranberries. Set aside.

In a mixing bowl, combine all of the dry ingredients. Stir together, to make sure

everything is distributed evenly.

Whisk together the eggs, Carb Countdown Dairy Beverage, melted butter, and

orange extract.

Make sure your oven is up to temperature before you add the wet ingredients to

the dry ingredients. When it is, pour the wet ingredients into the dry ingredients,

and stir the two together with a few swift strokes of your whisk or a spoon. Do not overmix! A few lumps are fine. Now add the

pecans and cranberries, and stir

just enough to incorporate into the batter. Spoon

into muffin cups, and bake for

20 minutes. Remove from pan to a wire rack to cool.

Yield: 12 muffins

Each with: 202 calories; 13 g fat; 18 g protein; 5 g

carbohydrate; 2 g dietary

fiber; 3 g usable carbo Carb count does not include

polyol sweetener.

Pumpkin Muffins

Just as with the Cranberry Nut Muffins, these

Pumpkin Muffins happened

because I couldn't get Pumpkin Bread to work out!

'/3 cup (50 g) almond meal

'/4 cup (25 g) gluten

'/4 cup (30 g) vanilla whey protein powder

'/4 teaspoon salt

'/4 cup (6 g) Splenda

1 teaspoon baking powder

'/2 teaspoon ground cinnamon

'/2 teaspoon ground nutmeg

'/2 cup (120 g) canned pumpkin

1 egg

2 tablespoons (30 g) butter, melted

'/4 teaspoon orange extract

'/3 cup (80 ml) Carb Countdown Dairy Beverage

'/2 cup (60 g) chopped pecans

Preheat oven to 400°F (200°C). Spray a 12-cup

muffin tin with nonstick cooking

spray, or, if you prefer, line it with paper muffin cups.

In a mixing bowl, measure all your dry ingredients.

Stir them together, to evenly

distribute ingredients.

Combine the canned pumpkin, egg, melted butter,

orange extract, and Carb

Countdown Dairy Beverage and whisk together.

Make sure your oven is up to

temperature before you take the next step!

Pour the wet ingredients into the dry ingredients and,

with a few swift strokes,

combine them. Stir just enough to make sure there

are no big pockets of dry

stuff; a few lumps are fine. Stir in the pecans quickly,

and spoon into prepared

muffin tin. Bake for 20 minutes; remove from pan to

a wire rack to cool.

Yield: 12 muffins

Each with: 119 calories; 8 g fat; 9 g protein; 3 g

carbohydrate; 6 g usable carbs.

Libby Sinback's Peach Sour Cream Muffins

Julie tested these muffins and said her whole family liked them!

1 cup (125 g) soy flour

1 cup (120 g) Designer Whey French vanilla protein powder

1 teaspoon baking powder

'/2 teaspoon salt

'/2 teaspoon baking soda

2 tablespoons (15 g) of stevia-FOS blend

1 cup (240 g) sour cream

'/2 cup (120 g) butter, melted

2 tablespoons (30 ml) cream

3 eggs

2 teaspoon orange peel

1 V2 cups (300 g) frozen peaches, slightly thawed, then diced

Preheat oven to 350°F (180°C).

Combine all dry ingredients, including the stevia-FOS blend, in a small bowl.

Combine sour cream, butter, cream, eggs, and orange peel in a larger mixing bowl.

Mix peaches in with dry ingredients, then fold into larger bowl with wet ingredi ents. Mix all ingredients until everything's wet, then pour into paper-lined muffin

tins, filling almost to the top.

Bake for 20 to 25 minutes at 350°F (180°C) degrees.

Yield: Makes 12 large muffins

Each with: 266 calories; 16 g fat; 19 g protein; 13 g carbohydrate; 2 g dietary

fiber; 11 g usable carbs.

Gingerbread Warnes

Really make Sunday breakfast something special!

Double or triple this recipe,

and you'll have extra waffles to freeze and reheat on

busy mornings. Tip-they'll

be a lot crispier and tastier if you reheat them in the

toaster than if you

microwave them.

1 cup almond meal

1 cup (120 g) vanilla whey protein powder

'/2 teaspoon salt

'/4 cup (6 g) Splenda

1 tablespoon (5 g) baking powder

2 teaspoons ground ginger

1 '/2 cups (360 ml) Carb Countdown Dairy Beverage

or 3j4 cup (180 ml)

heavy cream and 3/4 cup (180 ml) water

2 eggs

4 tablespoons (60 g) butter, melted

Start waffle iron heating.

Combine dry ingredients. In a glass measuring cup, whisk together the

carb-counting milk or cream and water and the eggs, then stir the butter into

them. Pour this into the dry ingredients, with a few quick strokes.

Ladle the batter into the waffle iron, and bake until done-my waffle iron has a

light that goes out when the waffle is ready, but follow the instructions for your

unit.

Serve with whipped cream.

Yield: 6 servings

Each with: 448 calories; 32 g fat; 35 g protein; 9 g carbohydrate; 3 g dietary

fiber, 6 g usable carbs.

Exceedingly Crisp Warnes

You have to separate eggs and all, but these waffles are worth it!

1j2 cup (60 g) almond meal

'/3 cup (40 g) vanilla whey protein powder

'/4 cup (30 g) oat flour

1j2 teaspoon baking powder

1 tablespoon (1.5 g) Splenda

'/4 teaspoon baking soda

3;4 cup (180 ml) buttermilk

1j4 cup (60 ml) Carb Countdown Dairy Beverage or half-and-half

6 tablespoons (90 ml) canola oil

1 egg

In one mixing bowl, combine the almond meal, vanilla whey, oat flour; baking

powder, Splenda, and baking soda. Stir the dry ingredients together.

Measure the buttermilk and Carb Countdown Dairy Beverage into a glass measuring cup. Add the canola oil.

Now's the time to plug in your waffle iron and get it heating; you want it to be

ready as soon as your batter is!

Separate that egg, making sure you don't get even a tiny speck of yolk in the

white. Add the yolk to the liquid ingredients. Put the white in a small, deep bowl,

and beat until stiff. Set aside.

Whisk all the liquid ingredients together, and pour them into the dry ingredients.

Mix everything quickly with a few quick strokes of your whisk. Mix only enough to

be sure all the dry ingredients are moistened.

Add about '/3 of the beaten egg white to the batter, and fold in gently, using a

rubber scraper. Then fold in the rest of the egg white.

Bake immediately, according to the directions that come with your waffle iron.

Serve with butter and sugar-free pancake syrup, cinnamon and Splenda, or low-sugar preserves.

Yield: How many waffles you get will depend on the size of your waffle iron; I got 6.

Each with: 282 calories; 21 g fat; 15 g protein; 9 g carbohydrate; 2 g dietary fiber, 7 g usable carbs.

Mary Lou Theisen's Best Low-Carb Warne

Our tester agrees these waffles are great.

4 ounces (115 g) cream cheese, softened

2 tablespoons vanilla whey protein powder

2 medium eggs (not large!)

1 teaspoon Splenda

1 teaspoon vanilla extract

'/2 teaspoon baking powder

Heat up waffle iron while mixing ingredients. Soften cream cheese in the microwave

for about 45 seconds. (You want the cream cheese nice and smooth.) Add the whey

protein powder, eggs, Splenda, vanilla extract, and baking powder. Mix until smooth.

Pour mixture into hot waffle iron (I do not grease the waffle iron, as the waffles come

out crispier without it). I heat the waffle for 2 minutes (this, of course, depends on

what kind of waffle maker you have). Take the waffle out; top with low-carb whipped cream and cinnamon or butter and sugar-free syrup.

Note: Our tester, Barbo Gold, who loved this recipe, suggests making these with

chocolate whey protein powder for a chocolate treat.

Yield: 2 servings

Each with: 326 calories; 25 g fat; 21 g protein; 4 g carbohydrate; trace dietary fiber;

4 g usable carbs.

Julie Sandell's Low-Carb Blueberry

Pancakes

Our tester, Ray Stevens, says these are not only quick

and easy, but good-looking

enough for company.

2 eggs

'/2 cup (115 g) whole-milk cottage cheese

1 scoop C/4 cup [30 g]) vanilla flavored whey protein

2 tablespoons (15 g) low-carb bake mix

'/2 teaspoon baking powder

Pinch of salt

'/2 cup (80 g) frozen blueberries

'1 2 Breads, Muffins, Cereals, Crackers, and Other

Grainy Things Mix all ingredients in order given.

Drop by large spoonfuls onto well-greased pan.

Cook until bubbly on top. Flip and cook a minute

longer.

Note: Julie says you can substitute a chopped-up

sugar-free chocolate bar for the

blueberries, and that sure sounds good to me!

Yield: Makes 3 servings of about 5 pancakes each.

Per serving: 183 calories; 5 g fat; 26 g protein; 8 g

carbohydrate; 2 g dietary

fiber; 6 g usable carbs.

Jill Taylor's Soy Pancakes

Our tester, Julie, says even her seven-year-old son Austin will eat these pancakes!

'/2 cup (60 g) soy flour

1j2 teaspoon baking powder

'/2 teaspoon Salt

'/2 teaspoon cinnamon

2 packets of artificial sweetener

1 teaspoon vanilla essence

'/2 cup (180 ml) water

2 eggs

Oil for cooking, or use a nonstick pan

Put all ingredients except the oil in a blender and mix until smooth. Let the

batter rest for 5 minutes. Heat a small skillet over medium to low heat until hot.

Add 1 to 2 tablespoons (15-30 ml) of the batter and cook until small bubbles

appear. Flip over and cook for a further 30 to 45 seconds.

Serve with fresh fruit, whipped cream, and sugar-free maple syrup.

Yield: Batter makes between 8 and 12 pancakes, depending on how big you make

them, so carb count per pancake will vary.

Each will have: 58 calories; 4 g fat; 3 g protein; 2 g carbohydrate; trace dietary

fiber; 2 g usable carbs.

Jeanette Wiese's Best Pancakes

I've Ever Had!

Our tester, Ray, calls these "hard to tell from the real thing."

1 scoop Designer Whey vanilla protein powder

1 scoop Designer Whey plain protein powder

'/3 cup (40 g) almond meal

2 teaspoons baking powder

Dash of cinnamon

1 ounce (30 g) cream cheese

2 eggs

2-4 teaspoons Splenda

'/4 cup (60 ml) oil

'/2 teaspoon vanilla extract

In one bowl, stir together protein powders, almond flour, baking powder, and

cinnamon. Soften cream cheese in microwave. In second bowl, whisk the eggs into

the cream cheese until well combined. Add sweetener, oil, and vanilla; whisk well.

Add egg mixture to dry ingredients, whisking until well combined.

Cook pancakes in a heavy skillet-it's best to use a nonstick skillet, but if you

don't have one, at least give it a good squirt of nonstick cooking spray. Then

heat it over medium-low heat. Use a V4 cup (60 ml) measuring cup, almost full,

for each pancake. The mixture will be pretty thick, so use a small spatula to help

drop the batter in a pan and spread it slightly to make round. Turn them carefully.

These will cook faster than regular pancakes, so keep an eye on them. Our tester,

Ray, points out that unlike "regular" pancakes, where you tell when the first side

is done by the bubbles around the edges, these have few bubbles. Instead, he

says, a "visible skin" forms on top of the pancake, and this is your signal to flip it.

Yield: Makes about 7 pancakes

Each with: 194 calories; 13 g fat; 17 g protein; 4 g carbohydrate; trace dietary fiber; 4 g usable carbs.

Oat Bran Pancakes

I like these for their grainy-cinnamony flavor. I eat 'em with butter and a little

cinnamon and Splenda.

'/2 cup (50 g) oat bran

1 cup (120 g) vanilla whey protein powder

1 V4 cups (155 g) almond meal

'/4 cup (6 g) Splenda

1 teaspoon baking powder

'/2 teaspoon baking soda

'/8 teaspoon salt

'/2 teaspoon cinnamon

2 cups (480 ml) buttermilk

2 eggs

In a medium-sized mixing bowl, combine all the dry ingredients, and stir to dis   tribute evenly. Measure the buttermilk in a glass measuring cup, and break the

eggs into it. Whisk the two together. Dump the buttermilk-and-egg mixture into the dry ingredients. Mix with a few quick strokes of the whisk, just enough to

make sure all the dry ingredients are incorporated. Heat a heavy skillet or griddle over a medium-high flame until a single drop of

water skitters around when dripped on the surface. Using a hot-pot holder,

remove from the heat just long enough to spray with nonstick cooking spray,

then return to the heat (the spray is flammable, so you don't want to be spraying

it at a hot burner!).

Pour about 2 to 3 tablespoons (30-45 ml) of batter at a time onto the hot

griddle. Cook until bubbles around the edges start to break and leave little holes,

then flip and cook other side.

Serve with butter and your choice of sugar-free pancake syrup, sugar-free jelly or

preserves, or cinnamon and Splenda.

Yield: 8 servings

Each with: 287 calories; 14 g fat; 32 g protein; 12 g carbohydrate; 3 g dietary fiber; 9 g usable carbs.

"Whole Wheat" Buttermilk Pancakes

'/2 cup (60 g) almond meal

'/2 cup (60 g) vanilla whey protein powder

'/4 cup (25 g) gluten

2 tablespoons (15 g) wheat germ

1 tablespoon (15 g) wheat bran

1 teaspoon baking powder

'/2 teaspoon baking soda

1 cup (240 ml) buttermilk

1 egg

2 tablespoons (30 g) butter, melted

In a mixing bowl, combine the dry ingredients. Stir
together so everything is
evenly distributed.

In a 2-cup (475 ml) glass measure, combine the
buttermilk, egg, and melted
butter; stir together.

Take a moment to set your big skillet or griddle over
medium heat, so it's ready
when you are.

Now, pour the wet ingredients into the dry

ingredients, and stir together with a

few swift strokes of your whisk.

When your skillet is hot enough that a single drop of

water sizzles and dances

around when dripped on the surface, you're ready to

cook. If your skillet doesn't

have a good nonstick surface, spray it with nonstick

cooking spray. (Turn off the

burner first, or remove the skillet from the burner

and turn away from the

flame-that spray is flammable!) Now you're ready to

fry your pancakes-I like

to use 2 tablespoons (30 ml) of batter per pancake.

Fry the first side until the

bubbles around the edges leave little holes when they

break, then flip and cook

the other side. Repeat until all the batter is used up!

Serve with butter and your choice of low-sugar

preserves, cinnamon and Splenda,

or sugar-free syrup-and don't think you're limited to maple-flavored pancake

syrup! Consider your favorite sugar-free coffee-flavoring syrup.

Yield: 5 servings (about 15 pancakes)

Each with: 233 calories; 13 g fat; 23 g protein; 7 g carbohydrate; 2 g dietary

fiber; 5 g usable carbs.

John Smolinski's Low-Carb Dutch Baby

A very popular puffy, oven-baked pancake.

3 ounces (85 g) cream cheese, softened

2 eggs

'/2 cup (120 ml) heavy cream

1 teaspoon vanilla

2 tablespoons (16 g) vanilla whey protein powder

'/2 teaspoon baking powder

1 teaspoon Splenda

1 -2 tablespoons (30 g) butter

Preheat your oven to 425 °F (220°C) degrees. While the oven is heating up, put

your cream cheese in a microwaveable mixing bowl, and microwave for 30 to 45

seconds to soften. Using an electric mixer or a whisk, beat the eggs, heavy cream,

vanilla, whey protein powder, baking powder, and Splenda in with the cream

cheese-incorporating plenty of air is a good thing here. Spray a 9" (22.5 cm) cake pan with nonstick cooking spray, then put 1 to 2

tablespoons (15-30 g) of

butter in the pan, and put it in your oven. Let the

butter melt, and then tilt the

pan to make sure the entire pan is coated with the

melted butter.

Pour the cream cheese mixture into the hot cake pan

(make sure you use oven

gloves to do this step and to put the cake pan back

into the oven). Bake for 10

to 12 minutes. You will have a fluffy, big Dutch

baby. Use a spatula to carefully

work it out of the pan. (You can flip the Dutch baby

out on one plate, then use

another plate to flip it back so that it faces up.) Top

with sour cream and warm

sugar-free maple syrup, butter and cinnamon-

Splenda, or a squeeze of lemon

juice and a sprinkle of Splenda.

Yield: 2 servings

Each with: 583 calories; 54 g fat; 21 g protein; 6 g carbohydrate; trace dietary fiber; 6 g usable carbs.

Graham Crackers

These are wonderful! Eat them as is, with some milk or reduced-carb dairy bev   erage, or spread them with a little cream cheese.

2;'3 cup (80 g) vanilla whey protein powder

2;'3 cup (80 g) almond meal

'/3 cup (35 g) oat bran

'/4 (25 g) wheat gluten

'/2 cup (50 g) wheat bran

'/2 cup (50 g) wheat germ

1 teaspoon baking powder

'/2 teaspoon baking soda

'/2 teaspoon salt

'/2 cup (120 ml) coconut oil

'/4 cup (50 g) granular polyol sweetener

'/4 cup (6 g) Splenda

1 1;2 teaspoons blackstrap molasses

'/2 cup (120 ml) Carb Countdown Dairy Beverage

In a mixing bowl, combine the vanilla whey protein powder, almond meal, oat bran, wheat gluten, wheat bran, wheat germ, baking powder, baking soda, and

salt. Stir to evenly distribute ingredients. Set aside.

Using an electric mixer, beat the coconut oil with the granular polyol sweetener,

Splenda, and blackstrap until the mixture is fluffy. Now beat in the dry ingredients

and the carb-reduced milk gradually, alternating which you add.

When all the dry ingredients and milk are beaten in, scrape the dough into a ball,

and refrigerate overnight. (This does something magical to the texture. I don't

understand it myself.)

Okay, next day you can pull your dough out of the fridge. Let it warm up for

15 or 20 minutes-while that's happening, you can preheat your oven to

350°F (180°C).

Divide the dough into two equal parts. Cover a cookie sheet with baking parch ment or a Teflon pan liner, and place one of the dough balls on it. Cover it with

another sheet of baking parchment, or another pan liner. Using a rolling pin, roll

" 8 Breads, Muffins, Cereals, Crackers, and Other Grainy Things out the dough between the two layers of parchment or liner, just a little thinner

than a commercial graham cracker. Peel off the top sheet, and use a pizza cutter

or a sharp, thin-bladed knife to score into squares. Prick each cracker 3 or 4

times with a fork.

Repeat this with the second dough ball, with a second set of parchment or pan

liners (you can use the same top sheet for both). Bake for about 15 to 20 minutes, or until browning a bit around the edges. Let cool, rescore, and break apart. Store in an airtight container.

Yield: 36 crackers

Each with: 68 calories; 4 g fat; 6 g protein; 3 g carbohydrate; 1 g dietary fiber,

2 g usable carbs. Carb count does not include polyol sweetener.

Parmesan Garlic Crackers

These are a variation on a cracker in 500 Low-Carb

Recipes-for you garlic fans,

and I know your name is Legion!

1 cup (225 g) sunflower seeds

'/2 cup (80 g) grated Parmesan cheese

1 1;2 teaspoons garlic powder

1 1;2 teaspoons onion powder

'/4 cup (60 ml) water

Preheat oven to 325 of (170°C).

Dump the sunflower seeds into your food processor,

with the S-blade in place.

Run the food processor until the seeds are ground

fine.

Add the Parmesan and the garlic and onion powders,

and pulse to combine.

Now turn on the processor, and pour in the water.

As soon as a soft dough

forms, turn it off.

Cover a baking sheet with baking parchment, and turn the dough out onto it.

Cover the dough with another sheet of baking parchment. Using a rolling pin, roll the dough out between the two layers of parchment, taking the time to get the dough seriously thin-so long as there are no holes, the thinner, the better.

Peel off the top sheet of parchment, and, using a thin-bladed sharp knife or a pizza cutter, score dough into diamonds or squares. Bake for about 30 minutes, or until evenly browned. Peel off the parchment, break along scored lines, and cool. Store in a tightly lidded container.

Yield: will depend on what size you make your crackers, of course. I make mine small, about the size of Wheat Thins, and get 6 dozen.

Each with: 14 calories; 1 g fat; 1 g protein; trace carbohydrate; trace dietary fiber;

no usable carbs. Heck, the whole batch has 34 g of carbs and 15 g of fiber, or a

usable carb count of 19 g!

Sunflower Wheat Crackers

These taste a bit like Wheat Thins, and would be

wonderful with dips-or just

by themselves!

1 cup (225 g) sunflower seeds

1/2 cup (50 g) wheat germ

1/4 cup (25 g) wheat bran

1/4 cup (25 g) oat bran

1/2 teaspoon salt

4 tablespoons (60 ml) canola oil

1/4 cup (60 ml) water

1 tablespoon (1.5 g) Splenda

In your food processor, using the S-blade, grind the

sunflower seeds until they're

a fine meal. Add the wheat germ, wheat bran, oat

bran, salt, and Splenda, and

pulse to mix.

Now pour in the oil, and pulse to mix that in. Finally,

add the water, and pulse to

make an evenly blended dough.

Cover a cookie sheet with baking parchment or a Teflon pan liner. Turn the dough out onto this. Cover with another sheet of parchment or another pan liner. Now roll the dough out through the top sheet, making it as thin as you can without making holes in it. It's really worth the time to make this seriously thin.

Using a knife with a thin, straight, sharp blade, or a pizza cutter, score the dough into squares or diamonds. I make mine about the size of Wheat Thins.

Bake for about 30 minutes, or until evenly golden. Rescore to help you separate the crackers without breaking them. Store in a tightly lidded container.

Yield: About 6 dozen small crackers.

Each with: 22 calories; 2 g fat; 1 g protein; 1 g carbohydrate; trace dietary fiber; 1 g usable carbo

Ruth Green's Cinnamon Crackers

A sweet, cinnamony, crunchy treat.

1 cup (150 g) whole roasted almonds

'/3 cup (40 g)vanilla-flavored whey protein powder

1 teaspoon cinnamon

2 tablespoons (3 g) Splenda

A scant '/2 cup (60 ml) water (take out 1 tablespoon water)

Preheat oven to 325 of (170°C).

Process the almonds in your food processor until finely ground. Then add all of

the dry ingredients and pulse the processor to blend. Now add the water;

process to mix. Using a rubber spatula, scrape bowl once.

Cover a cookie sheet with baking parchment. Turn the dough out onto this,

and cover with another sheet of parchment. Flatten with your hands or a rolling pin until quite thin. Peel off top sheet of parchment, and score into squares or

diamonds using your pizza cutter. (If the dough sticks to the top parchment as

you take it off and your crackers do not have a smooth top, reduce your water

slightly.)

Bake for about 25 minutes, until a cracker in the center feels firm when you tap

on it. It kind of makes a thumping sound.

Yield: The number of crackers per batch depends on how thin you like your

crackers and how big you cut them-I roll my batch out to be about 11 " x 11 "

(2Z5 x 2Z5 cm). Assuming you get 4 dozen crackers

...

Each cracker will have: 25 calories; 2 g fat; 2 g protein; 1 g carbohydrate; trace

dietary fiber; 1 g usable carbo

Ruth Green's Coconut Crackers

3/4 cup (115 g) whole roasted almonds

1/3 cup (40 g) vanilla-flavored whey protein powder

1/3 cup (25 g) unsweetened coconut flakes

2 tablespoons (3 g) Splenda

Scant V2 cup (60 ml) water

Process the almonds in your food processor until

finely ground. Then add all of

the dry ingredients and pulse the processor to blend.

Now add the water;

process to mix. Using a rubber spatula scrape bowl

once.

Cover a cookie sheet with baking parchment. Turn

the dough out onto this,

and cover with another sheet of parchment. Flatten

with your hands or a

rolling pin until quite thin. Peel off top sheet of

parchment, and score into

squares or diamonds using your pizza cutter. (If the

dough sticks to the top

parchment as you take it off and your crackers do not have a smooth top,

reduce your water slightly.)

Bake for about 25 minutes, until a cracker in the center feels firm when you tap

on it. It kind of makes a thumping sound. Ruth's note: "For a cool variation, use

lemon juice in place of the water."

Yield: The number of crackers per batch depends on how thin you like your

crackers and how big you cut them-I roll my batch out to be about " " x " "

(27.5 x 27.5 cm). Assuming you get 4 dozen crackers

...

Each cracker will have: 25 calories; 2 g fat; 2 g protein; , g carbohydrate; trace

dietary fiber; , g usable carbo

Buttermilk Drop Biscuits

You wouldn't believe how much trouble I had

coming up with a decent

low-carb biscuit! Everything I made either ran all

over the baking sheet or

was unpleasantly heavy. And I couldn't get a dough

that could be rolled out

and cut without sticking! Finally, I hit on the idea of

drop biscuits baked in

a muffin tin, and sure enough, it worked out great.

1 cup (125 g) almond meal

'/2 cup (125 g) rice protein

'/4 cup (25 g) gluten

2 tablespoons (30 g) butter

2 tablespoons (30 ml) coconut oil

'/2 teaspoon salt

2 teaspoons baking powder

'/2 teaspoon soda

3/4 cup (180 ml) buttermilk

Preheat oven to 475 °F (240°C)-the oven must be up to temperature before

you add the buttermilk to the dry ingredients, so do this first!

Put everything but the buttermilk into your food processor, with the S-blade in

place. Pulse food processor to cut in shortening-you want it evenly distributed

in the dry ingredients. Dump this mixture-it should have a mealy texture-into

a mixing bowl.

Spray a 12-cup muffin tin with nonstick cooking spray. Don't use paper muffin

cups; you want the browning you'll get from direct contact with the hot metal.

Check to make sure your oven is up to temperature-if it isn't, have a quick cup

of tea until it's hot. Now measure the buttermilk and pour it into your dry ingre   dients, and stir it in with

a few swift strokes-don't overmix; you just want to

make sure everything's evenly damp. This will make a soft dough. Spoon it into

your prepared muffin tin, smoothing the tops with the back of the spoon. Put in

the oven immediately, and bake for 10 to 12 minutes, or until golden on top.

Serve hot with butter, and, if you like, low-sugar preserves or sugar-free imitation

honey.

Yield: 12 biscuits

Each with: 153 calories; 10 g fat; 14 g protein; 4 g carbohydrate; 1 g dietary fiber,

3 g usable carbs.

Grainy Things Yeast Breads

Now we come to a few yeast-raised items. I offer these with a certain trepidation.

Of all the recipes in 500 Low-Carb Recipes, the yeast bread recipes have turned out to be the most problematic. They all work beautifully for me, or I wouldn't have included them. Many readers love them, but many others have written me com plaining that they can't get them to rise for love nor money. It's impossible to trou bleshoot, because there are so many variables involved-the problem could be a different brand of ingredients, the particular bread machine, hard versus soft water, dead yeast, the weather-all sorts of things. For what it's worth, some peo ple have had success using an extra teaspoon of yeast, while others find that mak ing sure that the yeast doesn't touch the liquid ingredients until the kneading starts makes a difference.

So there are just a few yeast-raised recipes here: dinner rolls and two loaf

breads. All call for a bread machine, and the quantities are for a 1-pound

(455 g) loaf, which is what my machine makes. If you have a bigger machine,

you'll just have to multiply.

125 ~ Dinner Rolls

These have a more elastic texture than carb-y dinner rolls; it comes from the

high protein content. (They're so high in protein, you could have a leftover roll

in the morning and call it breakfast.) But they come out wonderfully crusty and

have a good yeasty flavor. We had them for a holiday meal, and everyone liked

them, texture and all.

5 V2 ounces (155 ml) water

3 tablespoons (25 g) instant dry milk

3/4 cup (75 g) wheat gluten

3/4 cup (75 g) wheat protein isolate

'/2 cup (60 g) oat flour

2 tablespoons (30 g) butter

'/2 teaspoon salt

2 teaspoons active baker's yeast (one packet)

Put everything in your bread machine, in the order specified with your unit. Put

dough through two knead-and-rise cycles. Remove from machine.

Spray a 12-cup muffin tin with nonstick cooking spray.

Nip off bits of dough, and roll them into balls about 1" (2.5 cm) in diameter.

Place three dough balls in a clover-leaf configuration in each muffin tin.

Dough will be extremely elastic! Don't worry about trying to make each ball

completely smooth.

Let rolls rise for 60 to 90 minutes in a warm place.

Preheat oven to 350°F

(1S0°C), and bake rolls for 10 to 15 minutes, or until golden.

Serve with plenty of butter!

Yield: 12 rolls

Each with: 172 calories; 4 g fat; 26 g protein; S g carbohydrate; 1 g dietary fiber;

7 g usable carbs.

Maple Oat Bread

Sugar-free pancake syrup gives this bread a very special flavor.

7 ounces (205 ml) water

2 teaspoons sugar-free pancake syrup

3/4 cup (75 g) wheat gluten

1;2 cup (60 g) wheat protein isolate

1/4 cup (25 g) rolled oats

2 tablespoons wheat bran

1/4 cup (25 g) wheat germ

2 tablespoons (8 g) flax seed meal

1 tablespoon (8 g) oat flour

1/4 teaspoon salt

1 tablespoon (15 g) butter, softened

2 teaspoons active baker's yeast (one packet)

Put ingredients in bread machine in order given, unless the instructions with your

unit call for something quite different-then do it according to instructions!

Run bread machine through two knead-and-rise cycles. In my cheapie, low-tech, twelve-year-old bread machine, this means unplugging the machine when the first knead-and-rise cycle is through, plugging it back in, and hitting start again-but if your machine will automatically run two knead-and-rise cycles before baking, go with it. After the second rise, let the bread bake. Remove promptly from bread case when done, and cool before slicing and/or wrapping.

Yield: 12 slices

Each with: 133 calories; 3 g fat; 21 g protein; 5 g carbohydrate; 2 g dietary fiber; 3 g usable carbs. Carb count does not include the polyols in the sugar-free pan   cake syrup.

Poppy Seed Bread

This bread has a firm, close-grained texture that lends itself to thin slicing. It

also doesn't rise more than about 4" (10 cm), but I liked the flavor and texture

so much, I thought 1'd include it anyway. Don't eat poppy seeds if you're facing

a drug test! You run the risk of testing positive for opiates.

2j3 cup (160 ml) water

2j3 cup (70 g) gluten

3 tablespoons (20 g) wheat bran

3 tablespoons (25 g) oat flour

2/3 cup (80 g) almond meal

'/3 cup (35 g) wheat protein isolate

2 tablespoons (15 g) poppy seeds

3 tablespoons (25 g) powdered milk

1 tablespoon (15 g) butter, softened

2 teaspoons active baker's yeast

'/2 teaspoon salt

1 tablespoon (1.5 g) Splenda

Put everything in a bread machine in the order specified in the instructions that come with your unit. Run the dough through two knead-and-rise cycles, then bake. Remove from bread case immediately, and cool before slicing thin to serve.

Yield: About 12 slices

Each with: 154 calories; 7 g fat; 19 g protein; 6 g carbohydrate; 2 g dietary fiber; 4 g usable carbs.

'28 Breads, Muffins, Cereals, Crackers, and Other

Elizabeth Dean's

Next Best Thing to Cornbread

A decarbed version of Southern-style cornbread.

Butter for greasing pan

1 cup (125 g) almond meal

'/2 cup (60 g) soy flour

'/2 cup (60 g) natural-flavor whey protein powder

1 teaspoon stevia/FOS

1 tablespoon (5 g) baking powder

'/2 teaspoon salt

4 tablespoons (60 g) butter, melted

1 egg

'/2 cup (120 g) cream

'/2 cup (120 ml) water

'/2 teaspoon butter flavoring

Preheat oven to 400°F (200°C). Put a little butter in

an ovenproof skillet or 8" x

8" (20 x 20 cm) pan and place in oven until butter is

melted. Swirl melted butter

around to grease pan.

Combine dry ingredients in a large mixing bowl and mix well. In another bowl,

combine the remaining ingredients and mix well. Pour the liquid mixture all at

once into the dry mixture. Stir until combined, but do not overmix.

Pour the batter into the prepared pan and bake until top is golden and a tooth   pick inserted tests clean, about 15 to 20 minutes.

Yield: About 16 servings

Each will have: 120 calories; 7 g fat; 10 g protein; 5 g carbohydrate; trace dietary

fiber; 5 g usable carbs.

'29 ~ Sharyn Taylor's Granny's Spoon Bread

A decarbed version of this old-time favorite. Our tester, Ray, said, "I remember

my granny's homemade bread like this, and this tastes just like it."

2 cups (480 ml) soy milk (or substitute Carb Countdown Dairy Beverage)

3 tablespoons (45 g) butter, melted

2 heaping tablespoons (12 g) Atkins Bake Mix (or
other low-carb bake mix)

2 heaping tablespoons (20 g) corn meal

1 V2 teaspoons salt

2 teaspoons baking powder

4 slices stale low-carb bread, crumbled (Sharyn uses
Nature's Own

Wheat and Fiber, with 5 g per slice, but use the
lowest-carb bread

at your store.)

2 eggs, slightly beaten

Preheat oven to 425°F (220°C).

Grease an 8" (20 cm) cast-iron skillet, or a baking pan
of about the same size.

Heat milk and butter together (do not boil). Sift
together the dry ingredients.

Now stir in the heated milk and butter mixture, and
pour it over crumbled bread.

Stir in the eggs-mixture will be very soft.

Pour into pan and bake until brown.

Sharyn's Note: You can put 3 or 4 slices of bacon on top for added flavor. You could also add grated cheddar cheese to mixture before baking, if you want, but I like it just the way it is with butter on top.

Yield: Makes 8 servings

Each with: 112 calories; 8 g fat; 6 g protein; 6 g carbohydrate; 1 g dietary fiber; 5 g usable carbs.

Dean's Granola

Donna Hodach-Price writes, "When I announced my intent to begin cooking

low carb, my husband, Dean (who is really an 'old hippie') was very sad to hear

that my homemade, traditional granola was no longer on the 'acceptable' list.

He moped for months until I became more comfortable with low-carb cooking.

After a while, I went to work on developing my own low-carb version of his

favorite. While this pared-down version does not contain the 6 cups of rolled

oats or the full cup of honey, it is very tasty and relatively low carb! The first

time he tasted it, he gave it 'two thumbs up.'"

2 cups (100 g) All-Bran Extra Fiber Cereal

3 cups (210 g) shredded unsweetened coconut

2 cups (200 g) rolled oats

1 cup (125 g) pecan pieces

1 cup (225 g) raw pumpkin seeds (shelled)

1 cup (225 g) raw sunflower seeds (shelled)

1 cup (95 g) sliced almonds

1j2 cup (60 g) sesame seeds

1 cup (125 g) ground flax seeds

3 tablespoons (25 g) ground cinnamon

1j2 cup (60 g) vanilla whey protein powder

1 teaspoon salt

1 cup (240 g) butter (2 sticks), melted

1 1j2 cups (38 g) Splenda

Preheat oven to 350°F (180°C).

In very large bowl, combine all dry ingredients. Add Splenda to melted butter and

stir to combine. Pour butter mixture over dry ingredients and mix well.

Place mixture into two large, shallow baking pans and bake approximately 45 min   utes, stirring every 15 minutes or until lightly toasted. Do not allow to overbake!

Cool completely at room temperature before storing in tightly covered storage container.

Yield: 13 servings of 1 cup

Each with: 631 calories; 56 g fat; 15 g protein; 27 g carbohydrate; 12 g dietary fiber; 15 g usable carbs.

Almond-Parmesan Crust

This is a good "crumb crust" for savory dishes, like quiche.

1 V3 cups (200 g) almonds

'/2 cup (75 g) grated Parmesan cheese

6 tablespoons (90 g) butter, melted

1 tablespoon water

In your food processor, using the S-blade, grind the almonds until they're the

texture of cornmeal. Add the Parmesan cheese, and pulse to combine. Pour in the

butter and the water, and run the processor until a uniform dough is formed   you may need to stop the processor and run a butter knife around the bottom edge of the processor bowl halfway through.

Turn out into a 10" (25 cm) pie plate you've sprayed with nonstick cooking spray.

Bake at 350°F (180°C) for about 10 to 12 minutes. Cool before filling.

Yield: 8 servings

Each with: 238 calories; 22 g fat; 7 g protein; 5 g
carbohydrate; 3 g dietary fiber,
2 g usable carbs.

Pie Crust

Because rolling this pie crust out doesn't work well, you'll have to settle for one   crust pies. But that's lots better than no-crust pies! I'm very pleased with how the texture of this crust worked out; it's brittle and flaky, just like a pie crust

should be.

'/2 cup (60 g) almond meal

'/3 cup (40 g) rice protein

'/4 cup (25 g) gluten, wheat

1 pinch baking powder

'/2 teaspoon salt

'/3 cup (80 ml) coconut oil, chilled

1 tablespoon (15 g) butter, chilled

3 tablespoons (45 ml) ice water

, 32 Breads, Muffins, Cereals, Crackers, and Other Grainy Things Put the almond meal, rice protein, gluten, baking powder, and salt in your food processor, with the S-blade in place. Add the coconut oil and the butter, and pulse the food processor until the shortening is cut into the dry ingredients   it should be sort of mealy in texture.

Do use ice water, not just cold water-I put an ice cube in a cup and cover it

with water, and let the water sit for a minute. Now add 1 tablespoon of this

water, pulse the food processor briefly, then repeat 2 more times, with the other

2 tablespoons of water.

I find that pressing this crust into place works better than rolling it out. Dump

out the dough into a 9" (22.5 cm) pie plate, and press it into place evenly

across the bottom and up the sides; then crimp the top rim, if you want to be

spiffy about it.

You can now bake your pie shell empty and use it for any recipe that calls for a prebaked pie shell, or you can fill and bake it according to any recipe that calls

for an unbaked pie shell. If you want to prebake your pie shell, preheat your oven

to 450°F (230°C). Prick the bottom of the pie shell all over with a fork, then add

a layer of dried beans, marbles, or clean, round pebbles-this is to keep your pie

shell from buckling. Bake for 10 minutes, take it out of the oven, and remove the

beans, marbles, or pebbles, dealing gingerly with any that may have embedded

themselves a bit. Return the crust to the oven for another 3 to 5 minutes, then

cool and fill.

Yield: 8 servings

Each with: 194 calories; 15 g fat; 15 g protein; 3 g carbohydrate; 1 g dietary

fiber; 2 g usable carbs.

133 chapter f i v e

The Ultimate Fauxtatoes

I'm not crazy about Ketatoes by themselves, but added to pureed-cauliflower Fauxtatoes, they add a potato-y flavor and texture that is remarkably convincing!

'/2 head cauliflower

'/2 cup (25 g) Ketatoes mix

'/2 cup (120 ml) boiling water

1 tablespoon (15 g) butter

Salt and pepper

Trim the bottom of the stem of your cauliflower, and whack the rest of the head into chunks. Put them in a microwaveable casserole with a lid. Add a couple of tablespoons of water, cover, and microwave on high for 8 to 9 minutes.

While that's happening, measure your Ketatoes mix and boiling water into a mix ing bowl, and whisk together.

When the microwave beeps, pull out your cauliflower-it should be tender. Drain it well, and put it in either your food processor, with the S-blade in place, or in your blender. Either way, puree the cauliflower until it's smooth. Transfer the pureed cauliflower to the mixing bowl, and stir the cauliflower and Ketatoes together well. Add the butter, and stir till it melts. Salt and pepper to taste, and serve.

Yield: 4 servings

Each with: 140 calories; 5 g fat; 10 g protein; 14 g carbohydrate; 8 g dietary fiber; 6 g usable carbs.

1 large chipotle chile canned in adobo, minced;

reserve 1 teaspoon sauce

1j2 cup (60 g) shredded Monterey Jack cheese

1 batch The Ultimate Fauxtatoes (page 136)

Stir the minced chipotle, a teaspoon of the adobo

sauce it was canned in, and

the shredded cheese into the Ultimate Fauxtatoes.

Serve immediately!

Yield: 4 servings

Each with: 193 calories; 10 g fat; 14 g protein; 14 g

carbohydrate; 8 g dietary

fiber; 6 g usable carbs.

Nancy O'Connor's

Creamy Garlic-Chive Fauxtatoes

Miss baked potatoes with sour cream and chives? Try this.

4 cups (600 g) fresh cauliflower

1/2 cup (115 g) cream cheese with chives

2 tablespoons (30 g) butter

1 clove garlic, crushed

Salt and pepper to taste

Put your cauliflower in a microwaveable casserole with a lid. Add a couple of

tablespoons water, cover, and nuke it on high for 8 minutes or so, until tender.

Blend cooked cauliflower in food processor with the cream cheese, butter, and

garlic. Salt and pepper to taste, then serve.

Yield: 3 servings

Each with: 236 calories; 20 g fat; 5 g protein; 10 g carbohydrate; 3 g dietary

fiber; 7 g usable carbs.

137 @) Bubble and Squeak

This is my decarbed version of a tradition Irish dish-
and very tasty, too!

1 tablespoon (15 g) butter

2 cups (150 g) shredded cabbage

1 medium carrot, shredded

3j4 cup (120 g) chopped onion

1 batch The Ultimate Fauxtatoes (page 136)

'/2 cup (60 g) shredded cheddar cheese

Melt the butter in your big, heavy skillet and saute the
veggies until the onion is

turning translucent and the cabbage has softened a
bit.

Spray a 6-cup (1 .4 L) casserole dish with nonstick
cooking spray. Spread '/3 of the

Fauxtatoes on the bottom, then make a layer of 1j2
the cabbage mixture. Repeat the

layers, then finish with a layer of Fauxtatoes. Top
with the cheese. Bake at 350°F

(180°C) for 45 minutes, then serve, scooping down through all the layers.

Yield: 6 servings

Each with: 167 calories; 9 g fat; 10 g protein; 14 g carbohydrate; 6 g dietary fiber;

8 g usable carbs.

Pork Rind Stuffing

This is remarkably like cornbread stuffing! By the way, Trish runs a website that

carries a few hard to find specialty products-

www.lowcarber.com

1 cup (120 g) chopped celery

'/4 cup (40 g) chopped onion

Salt and pepper, to taste

Poultry seasoning, to taste

1 packet Splenda or other sweetener

2 tbsp (30 g) butter

1j4 cup (60 ml) cream

3 '/2 ounces (105 ml) chicken broth (about 1j4 can)

10 ounces (280 g) pork rinds, crushed

4 eggs

, 38 Hot Vegetables and Other Sides Saute celery, onion, salt, pepper, poultry seasoning, sweetener, and butter in a fry ing pan until transparent and tender. Add other ingredients and mix together until the pork rinds are coated and moist. Put into baking dish and bake for 35 to 50

minutes until set like regular bread stuffing. Feel free to add more eggs or cream to

get the texture you are used to. Some people also add mushrooms, sage, sausage,

or oysters.

Yield: 8 servings

Each will have: 276 calories; 18 g fat; 25 g protein; 2 g carbohydrate; trace dietary

fiber; 2 g usable carbs.

Hellzapoppin Cheese "Rice"

Another recipe I've adapted from the funniest

cookbook ever written,

The I Hate To Cook Book, by Peg Bracken. And

truly fabulous it is, too.

'/3 cup (55 g) cooked wild rice

4 eggs

1 cup (240 ml) Carb Countdown Dairy Beverage

1j4 cup (60 g) minced onion

1 tablespoon (15 ml) Worcestershire sauce

1 teaspoon salt

'/2 teaspoon dried thyme

'/2 teaspoon dried marjoram

3 1j3 cups (500 g) shredded cauliflower (about '/2

head)

1 pound (455 g) grated sharp cheddar cheese

1 10-ounce (280 g) box frozen chopped spinach,

thawed

You need to have your wild rice cooked before you

start. Make more than you need

for this recipe and stash it in a snap-top container in the freezer; next time you'll

have it on hand!

Beat the eggs till they're foamy, then whisk in the Carb Countdown Dairy Beverage,

onion, Worcestershire, salt, thyme, and marjoram. Now, stir in the raw cauli-rice, the

wild rice, the cheese, and the spinach. Stir till everything is well combined.

Pour the whole thing into a casserole dish you've sprayed with nonstick cooking

spray, and bake it at 375 °F (190°C) for 35 to 40 minutes.

Yield: 6 servings

Each with: 409 calories; 30 g fat; 27 g protein; 10 g carbohydrate; 3 g dietary fiber;

7 g usable carbs.

'39 ~ Japanese Fried "Rice"

1;2 head cauliflower, shredded

2 eggs

1 cup (75 g) snow pea pods, fresh

2 tablespoons (30 g) butter

1;2 cup (80 g) diced onion

2 tablespoons (16 g) shredded carrot

3 tablespoons (45 ml) soy sauce

Salt and pepper

Put the shredded cauliflower in a microwaveable casserole with a lid, add a couple

of tablespoons of water, cover, and microwave on high for 6 minutes.

While that's happening, scramble the eggs and pour them into a skillet you've

sprayed with nonstick cooking spray, over medium-high heat. As you cook the

eggs, use your spatula to break them up into pea-sized bits. Remove from skillet

and set aside.

Remove the tips and strings from the snow peas, and snip into '/4" (6.25 mm) lengths. (By now the microwave has beeped-take the lid off your cauliflower

or it will turn into a mush that bears not the slightest resemblance to rice!)

Melt the butter in the skillet, and saute the pea pods, onion, and carrot for

2 to 3 minutes.

Add the cauliflower, and stir everything together well. Stir in the soy sauce,

and cook the whole thing, stirring often, for another

5 to 6 minutes. Salt and

pepper a bit, and serve.

Yield: 5 servings

Each with: 91 calories; 6 g fat; 4 g protein; 5 g carbohydrate; 1 g dietary fiber;

4 g usable carbs.

Lonestar "Rice"

1/2 head cauliflower, shredded

1j 4 cup (40 g) chopped onion

1 cup (100 g) sliced mushrooms

1/2 cup (40 g) snow pea pods, fresh, cut in 1j2" (1.25 g) pieces

1 tablespoon (15 ml) olive oil

1 tablespoon (15 g) butter

1/4 teaspoon chili powder

2 teaspoons beef bouillon granules or concentrate

Put the cauliflower in a microwaveable casserole with a lid. Add a couple of

tablespoons of water, cover, and microwave on high for 6 minutes.

While that's cooking, saute your onions, mushrooms, and snow peas in the

olive oil and butter, in your big skillet. I like to use the edge of my spatula to

break up the mushrooms into smaller pieces, but leave the slices whole if you like them better that way-up to you. When the mushrooms have changed

color and the snow peas are tender-crisp, drain your cooked caul i-rice, and stir it

in. Add the chili powder and beef bouillon, and stir to distribute the seasonings

well, then serve.

Yield: 3 servings

Each with: 99 calories; 9 g fat; 2 g protein; 5 g carbohydrate; 1 g dietary fiber;

4 g usable carbs.

Venetian "Rice"

This is rich tasting and slightly piquant.

'/2 head cauliflower

1 tablespoon (15 ml) olive oil

2 tablespoons (30 g) butter

1 cup (lOa g) sliced mushrooms

3 anchovy fillets, minced

1 clove garlic, crushed

3 tablespoons (30 g) grated Parmesan cheese

Run the cauliflower through the shredding blade of

your food processor. Put it in

a microwaveable casserole with a lid, add a couple of

tablespoons of water, cover,

and nuke on high for 5 to 6 minutes. When it's done,

uncover immediately!

Combine the olive oil and butter in your big heavy

skillet over medium heat,

swirling together as the butter melts. Add the

mushrooms and saute until they're

soft and changing color. If your mushroom slices are quite large,you may want to

break them up a bit with the edge of your spatula as you stir.

When the mushrooms are soft, stir in the minced anchovies and garlic. Add the

cauli-rice, undrained-that little bit of water is going to help the flavors blend.

Stir well to distribute all the flavors.

Stir in the Parmesan, and serve.

Yield: 3 to 4 servings

Each will have: 148 calories; 10 g fat; 4 g protein; 2 g carbohydrate; 1 g dietary

fiber; 1 g usable carbo

Cheesy Cauliflower

4 cups (600 g) cauliflower florets, cut 1;2" (1.25 cm) thick

'/3 cup (50 g) chopped onion

'/2 green bell pepper, diced

2 tablespoons (30 ml) olive oil

4 cloves garlic, crushed

'/2 teaspoon dried basil

'/2 cup (120 ml) half-and-half

1 cup (120 g) shredded Monterey Jack cheese

Put your cauliflower in a microwaveable casserole with a lid. Add a tablespoon or two of water, cover, and nuke on high for 7 minutes. While that's happening, start the onion and pepper sauteing in the olive oil, in a large heavy skillet over medium-high heat.

By the time the microwave goes beep, your pepper and onion should be getting soft. Drain the cauliflower, and dump it into the skillet. Stir everything around together. Stir in the garlic, and saute for another minute or two.

Now stir in the basil, half-and-half, and shredded cheese. Keep stirring till the

cheese is melted. Let the whole thing cook for another minute or two, then serve.

Yield: 5 servings

Each with: 195 calories; 15 g fat; 8 g protein; 8 g carbohydrate; 2 g dietary fiber;

6 g usable carbs.

Gratin of Cauliflower and Turnips

2 1;2 cups (375 g) turnip slices

2 1;2 cups (375 g) sliced cauliflower

1 1;2 cups (360 ml) carb-counting milk

'/4 cup (60 ml) heavy cream

3/4 cup (90 g) blue cheese, crumbled

'/2 teaspoon pepper

'/2 teaspoon salt

1 teaspoon dried thyme

Guar or xanthan (optional)

'/4 cup (40 g) Parmesan cheese

Combine the turnips and cauliflower in a bowl, making sure they're pretty evenly interspersed.

In a saucepan, over lowest heat, warm the carb-counting milk and heavy cream.

When it's hot, add the blue cheese, pepper, salt, and thyme. Stir with a whisk until the cheese is melted. It's good to thicken this sauce just slightly with your guar or xanthan shaker.

Spray a casserole dish with nonstick cooking spray.
Put about '/3 of the
cauliflower and turnip slices in the dish, and pour 1;3
of the sauce evenly over
them. Make two more layers of vegetables and sauce.
Sprinkle the Parmesan
cheese over the top. Bake at 375 OF (190°C) for 30
minutes.

Yield: 6 servings

Each with: 142 calories; 10 g fat; 7 g protein; 8 g
carbohydrate; 3 g dietary fiber;
5 g usable carbs.

Lightning Source UK Ltd.
Milton Keynes UK
UKHW022000030621
384904UK00002B/529